To An AMAZING TEACHER

Made in the USA
Las Vegas, NV
13 May 2021

22940038R00061